Warming Up for Cello

book one

by Cassia Harvey

CHP120
ISBN: 978-1-932823-19-6

6403 N. 6th Street
Philadelphia, PA 19126
www.charveypublications.com

Less-advanced (A) pages are structured so that they can be played together with more-advanced (B) pages.

Contents

Warmups in G major

Daily Exercise (A)

Cassia Harvey

March (A)

L. Mozart, arr. Harvey

Warming Up for Cello, Book One

Daily Exercise (B)

March (B)

L. Mozart, arr. Harvey

Finger Workout (A)

Sonata (A)

Cimarosa, arr. Harvey

Warming Up for Cello, Book One

8

Finger Workout (B)

Sonata (B)

Cimarosa, arr. Harvey

Finger Twister (A)

Dill Pickle Rag (A)

Johnson, arr. Harvey

12

Finger Twister (B)

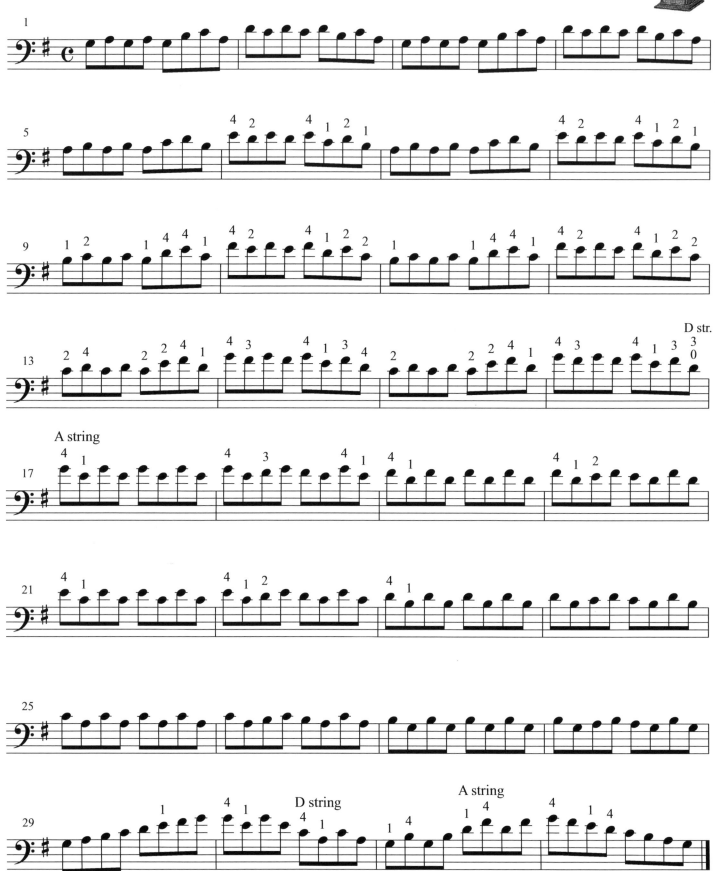

Dill Pickle Rag (B)

Johnson, arr. Harvey

Warmups in D major

Daily Exercise (A)

Variations on a Theme (A)

Romberg, arr. Harvey

16

Daily Exercise (B)

Variations on a Theme (B)

Romberg, arr. Harvey

Warming Up for Cello, Book One

Finger Workout (A)

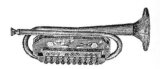

Rondo (A)

Mozart, arr. Harvey

Finger Workout (B)

Rondo (B)

Mozart, arr. Harvey

Warming Up for Cello, Book One

22

Finger Twister (A)

Warming Up for Cello, Book One

©2004 C. Harvey Publications All Rights Reserved.

Miss Ratray's Reel (A)

Trad., arr. Harvey

Finger Twister (B)

Miss Ratray's Reel (B)

Trad., arr. Harvey

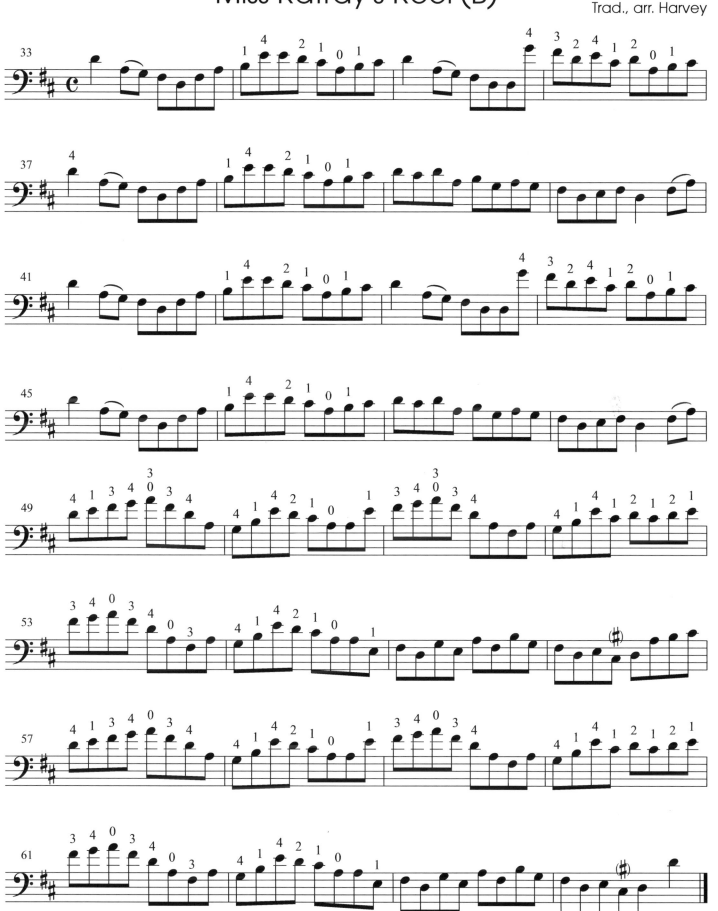

Warmups in C major

Daily Exercise (A)

Mason's Apron (A)

Trad., arr. Harvey

Daily Exercise (B)

Mason's Apron (B)

Trad., arr. Harvey

Finger Workout (A)

Bourree (A)

Bach, arr. Harvey

Finger Workout (B)

Bourree (B)

Bach, arr. Harvey

Finger Twister (A)

Grazioso (A)

Cimarosa, arr. Harvey

Finger Twister (B)

Grazioso (B)

Cimarosa, arr. Harvey

Warmups in F major

Daily Exercise (A)

Variation (A)

Paganini, arr. Harvey

40

Daily Exercise (B)

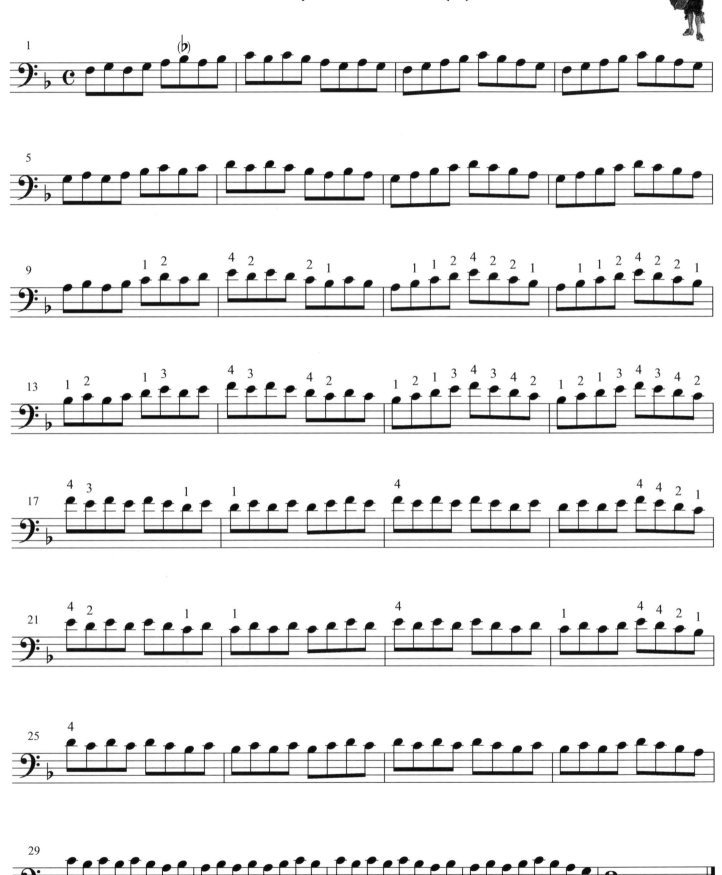

Variation (B)

Paganini, arr. Harvey

Finger Workout (A)

Allegro (A)

Paxton, arr. Harvey

43

Finger Workout (B)

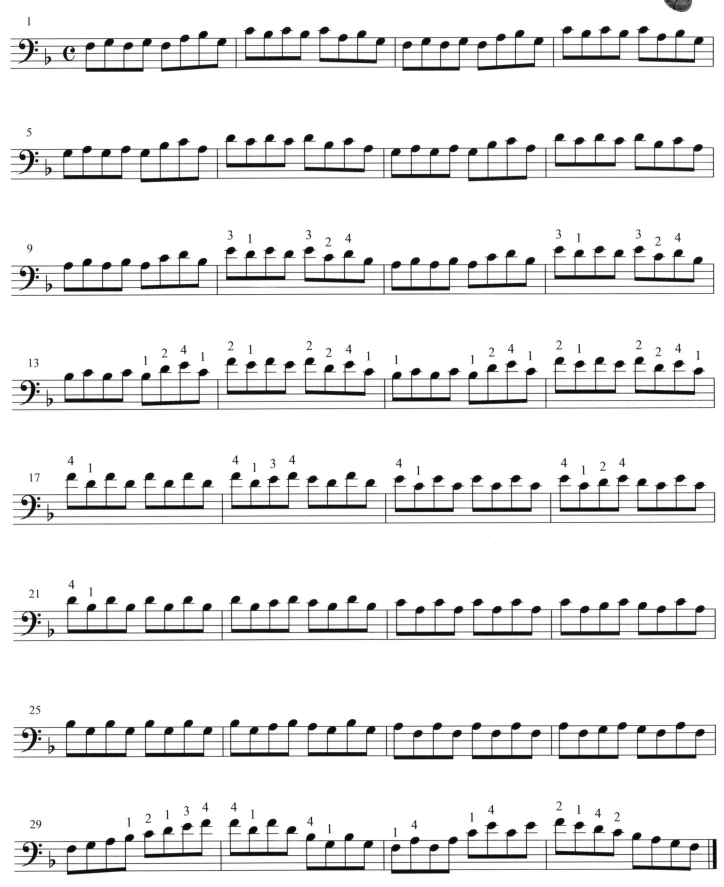

Allegro (B)

Paxton, arr. Harvey

Finger Twister (A)

The Dashing Sergeant (A)

Trad., arr. Harvey

Finger Twister (B)

The Dashing Sergeant (B)

Trad., arr. Harvey

Warming Up for Cello, Book One

Note: The Suite is broken up into sections in this study book. The complete Suite is at the back of the book.

Suite No. 1: Prelude
Part One: Measures 1-4 (Bowing #1)

Suite by J. S. Bach
Exercises by Cassia Harvey

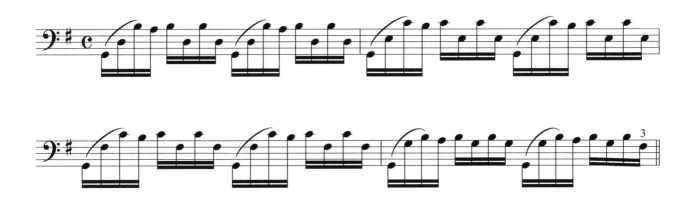

Double Stops for Intonation
Measures 1-4